Mystie's Activities for

Bereaved Children

Grades 3-5

Utilizing
For the Love of Emrys

KIDS' GRIEF RELIEF

Hi, I'm Mystie.
What's
Dragon - You - Down ?

www.KidsGriefRelief.org

A 501(c)(3) NonProfit

Grief Support to Empower Bereaved Children

My Special Activity Booklet about

_____ and me.

Activity 1A

MY FAMILY MEMBERS

Circle the ones you live with

My special person who died: _____

Hi Kids!
My name is Mystie. I'm a mystical, magical dragonfly from a far away planet.

TIME TO SHARE

What's your name?

What grade are you in?

How old are you?

Who died?

Share your cover picture with your group.

Activity 2

Are you feeling dragged—down because someone you love has died?

I felt dragged—down when my best friend suddenly died. I knew I would never see him again. It felt awful. I couldn't even fly.

I was feeling

GRIEF.

When I first flew to Earth, I thought Earth dragonflies lived forever like the dragonflies on Nilrem, where I come from.

So when I met Darvy, the Earth dragonfly, I thought we would be friends for a long time. But I was wrong. Earth dragonflies have a short life.

Darvy and I had so much fun together! We flew wildly all over the marsh at the edge of the beach, where we lived. We laughed and played all day long. I loved being with him!

Then one day while we were playing dragonfly tag, he died. He suddenly stopped flying and fell to the ground. I was shocked. I felt terrible. I couldn't believe what happened.

We had a funeral, and buried him near a special rock where we used to sit and talk. I cried and cried.

I had a lot of different feelings. Some of the feelings are listed on the next page. What are YOU feeling?

Activity 3B

Circle the words that tell about how you feel:

Mad

Scared

Guilty

Very
Sad

Shocked

Upset

Glad

Angry

Worried

Lonely

Confused

Distracted

Frustrated

_____

Can you share aloud
why you circled
those words?

TIME TO
SHARE

For example,
"I feel worried because my dad
is very sad like me."

Everyone grieves differently.
There's no right or wrong way.
You are grieving your way. The
other students in your group are
grieving the way they need to.

Don't
talk to students
outside of your group about
what's going on within your group.
Whatever is said, stays in your group.
It's confidential.

Write your name on the line below, if you
agree to this. Also write today's date.

_____

Activity 5

When I was feeling dragged—down about Darvy's death, the beautiful colors in my wings were all muddied up. I had so many feelings.

-----------What colors show your feelings?-----------

For example, what color shows you're sad? Blue? Gray?

What color shows you're upset? You're worried?

Would you color in my wings to show how you feel?

©2014 Kids' Grief Relief

You might also have pains in your body, like a stomach ache or head ache. You might feel extra tired. It's good to talk about how your body is feeling, too.

How does your body feel?

TIME TO SHARE

My friend Lark, the dolphin, helped me a lot when I was grieving over Darvy.

Activity 7

In the heart below, write the names of family members, friends and teachers, who can help you and answer your questions about the death of your special person.

Hi Kids! How are you feeling today?

Today I am feeling_____

_____

Read:

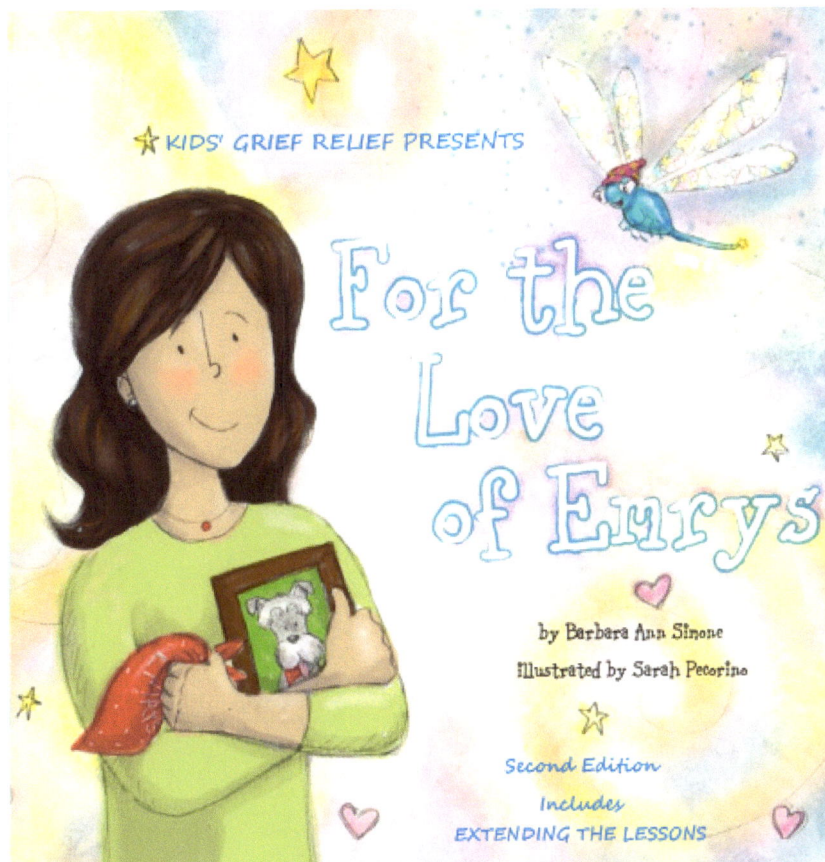

At the end of her story, Christina feels a lot better. She knows Emrys will always be in her heart. She has lots of love to share with others; she'll love them for the rest of her life.

Activity 10A

Now it's your turn to tell your story about what happened when your loved one died. You can either speak it aloud, or write it down and share what you've written.

TIME TO
SHARE

To guide you, Christina tells certain parts of her story, so you can tell the same part of YOUR story.

Before Emrys died, we had so much fun together!

We played in the park and jogged all over the neighborhood. He sat in my lap or next to me all the time.

Describe your relationship with your special person before their death.

Emrys had a disease. One day he suddenly died right in front of me. I was very sad and VERY upset. I cried all the way to the veterinarian's office, where I took his dead body. When I finally went home, everything felt wrong.

What happened the day your special person died?

Emrys was cremated. I believe I honored him alot by spreading his ashes all over the neighborhood where he and I used to run.

How did you honor your special person? Was there a funeral? Did you have a special meal? Was your special person cremated? Where are their ashes?

Activity 10C

My mom and my friends were very sad that Emrys had died.

They loved him too. They were worried about how I was going to be without him. Dr. Bacon was also very sad because he thought Emrys was a great dog.

How did the rest of your family react to the death of your special person?

The worst part of Emrys dying was that he died in front of me. That was a hard thing to handle, but I was brave and stayed with him as he died.

What was the worst thing that happened when your special person died?

I learned that love lives inside me. The love I shared with Emrys started in my heart. Now I choose to share that Love with other people and other animals.

What did you learn from your experience?

Activity 10D

Were you a good listener when the other students were telling their story? I hope so!

You had the opportunity to practice
COMPASSION.

Compassion comes from your loving heart. It's a warm feeling of understanding that someone is hurting. You take the time to listen to someone tell about their hurt. Listening with a loving heart helps a lot.

I showed COMPASSION for
(list the members of your grief group)

Activity 11

You can also practice Compassion
by speaking words which come from your heart.

Everyone grieves differently.
But having someone care helps a person
who is feeling grief.

Here are some ideas of what to say.
Read each one to yourself,
then choose one to say tosomeone else

"Your _____loved you a lot. I know you're going to miss her. I bet you have lots of great memories about her.

"I'm sorry to hear about the death of _____. You must miss him very much."

"I know you feel really sad about _____dying. It's okay to feel sad and upset about it."

"I'm sorry to hear abou the death of your _____. I guess this is a hard time for you."

"I feel sad to hear about the death of your _____. I'm here if you need someone to talk to."

Activity 12

Hi Kids! How are you feeling today?

Today I am feeling_____

_____

On the next page there's a game to play.
You each have your own board.

Directions:
1. Choose a marker.
2. Decide the order of players.
3. First person rolls the dice and moves that many spaces along their board.
4. Read the question on the square. If you can answer it, speak it aloud. Circle the number on the square.
5. If it's a question you can't answer, put an X on the square and skip over it the next time around.
6. Play until you reach or pass the last square.
7. Claim your prize once you finish !

Remember to practice
Compassion
when you play this game!

Activity 13A

1 What is the first and last name of your special person ?	**2** Did your special person teach you anything ?	**3** Do you know your special person's birthday ? (Day/Month/Year)	**4** Was your special person buried or cremated ?	**5** Did your special person like to wear jewelry ? What kind ?
6 Describe a special holiday spent with your special person.	**7** Tell about the last time you saw your special person.	**8** What name did your special person call you ?	**9** Tell about a funny moment with your special person.	**10** Describe a trip you took with your special person.
11 Tell about what kind of clothes your special person liked to wear.	**12** Tell about an object that reminds you of your special person.	**13** What kind of music did your special person enjoy ?	**14** What kind of movies did your special person like to watch ?	**15** Did your special person ever have a pet ?
16 Did your special person have a favorite saying - what was it ?	**17** Tell about a sad memory with your favorite person.	**18** Tell about some of the people who loved your special person.	**19** What one thing always makes you think about your special person ?	**20** What's your favorite photo of your special person ? Describe it.
21 Tell about something your special person loved to do.	**22** What time of day do you feel "dragged-down" over the death of your special person ?	**23** What's the one thing you will miss MOST about your special person ?	**24** Do you feel peaceful about the way your special person was buried ? Why ?	**25** Tell about a gift you gave your special person.

Activity 13B

My favorite memory of my friend Darvy the earth dragonfly, is playing tag with him.
He was very fast, but I usually outflew him!
We laughed and laughed as we played together.
I think a lot about Darvy.

I wonder what other adventures we could have had together.

I try to remember that he is happy in dragonfly heaven.

I understand why he died, though I don't like it.

I want to always remember how he made me laugh.

I learned a lot about myself after he died.

I am a mystical, magical dragonfly who misses my best friend so much!

TIME TO SHARE

I wonder _____.

I try _____.

I understand _____.

I want _____.

I learned _____.

I am _____.

Activity 14

I believe Darvy's spirit is somewhere
in dragonfly heaven.
Christina believes Emrys' spirit is
in heaven, too.

Where do you believe your
special person's spirit is?
Draw a picture of what you
think it looks like.

Activity 15

Here's a picture of Christina holding a picture of her pet dog Emrys, who died.

She's also holding his bandanna, which she saved to remind her of him.

What special things do you have to remind yourself about your special someone who died? Make a list.

⭐ 1

⭐ 2

⭐ 3

⭐ 4

⭐ 5

⭐ 6

Activity 16

Hi Kids! How are you feeling today?

Today I am feeling _____

Look at the mobile of me. Can you bend my wings to show everyone how you've been feeling the past week?

When you're grieving over someone, parts of you may be happy, yet parts may be still sad or upset.

Use my four wings to show your feelings.

Activity 17

Through her grief, Christina learned that the love in her heart is changeless. She will always love Emrys. She loved him when he was alive, and continues to love him even though he is gone.

Your love for your special person will be inside your heart forever, too.

Look at the heart below.

On the left side of the heart, write about how you showed love for your special person before he/she died.

On the right side write or draw pictures of how you show you still love him/her.

Loving yourself, by doing things you enjoy can help you move through grief.

Think about ways you can help yourself to feel better. You can draw pictures or write down your ideas.

When I feel sad I can

When I feel worried I can

When I feel scared I can

When I feel angry I can

When I feel upset I can

When I feel _____ I can

Activity 19A

What's your favorite thing to do?
Close your eyes for a moment,
and pretend you are doing it.

Now, color and decorate my wings to show how
you feel when you're doing your favorite thing.

I know you can't fly
like me, but you can
feel like you're flying,
when you're doing
something you
really enjoy.

Here's another way to help yourself
when you're feeling dragged—down.

It's all about BREATHING.

When you take the time to control how you
breathe, you can help yourself handle some of
the dragged—down emotions of grief.

You will feel more relaxed and calm. Your
body gets the air it needs to calm itself down.

That feels good.

Activity 20

Hi Kids! How are you feeling today?

Today I am feeling

_____

When I was grieving over the death of Darvy, the earth dragonfly, Lark reminded me that my thoughts had a lot to do with how I was feeling.

The more positive my thoughts, the better I felt.

The following is what Lark shared with me. →

I am excited to share it with you.

Activity 21A

1. BECOME AWARE OF WHAT YOU'RE THINKING.

2 MAKE THE CHOICE TO GET RID OF ANY DRAGGED—DOWN THOUGHTS. THROW THEM AWAY!

3 FOCUS ON THE LOVE IN YOUR HEART TO THINK NEW THOUGHTS THAT MAKE YOU FEEL BETTER.

Activity 21B

Here are some "Dragged—Down" thoughts you might be thinking. Are any of these familiar to you? If so, trace over the arrow with your marker or crayon.

I wish I could change what happened.

It's terrible that I will never see _____ again.

I keep thinking about how _____ died.

What if someone else dies?

My life is now all messed up.

I should have been nicer to _____.

If only I could have _____, maybe _____ wouldn't have died.

I don't think I will ever be happy again.

IT'S NOT FAIR!

Activity 22

©2014 Kids' Grief Relief

Which Dragged—Down thoughts
are you ready to get rid of?

Write them on the arrows below.
Then count to three, take a deep breath,
and THROW THEM AWAY!

And keep them in the trash!

Activity 23

Here are some of my
Dragon—Fly thoughts
that you can think as you focus on the
<u>love in your heart.</u>

Can you say these aloud?

1. I am brave.

2. I am smart enough to understand
   what happened.

3. It feels good to talk to others about
   what happened.

4. I have my own unique feelings
   about death.

5. I have special memories of _____
   that I will always treasure.

6. I like who I am.

7. I am grateful for all the people who
   love me.

8. I am a powerful kid!

Activity 24

Write a Dragon—Fly thought for each of the four sides of the frame below. Draw a picture of yourself in the frame.

Hi Kids! How are you feeling today?

Today I am feeling _____

Things have changed in your life. Can you share some things that are different since the death of your loved one?

Can you share some things that have stayed the same?

TIME TO SHARE

What are some things you're looking forward to this coming year?

You've done a great job learning how to deal with the death of your loved one. You are very brave!

Here are some statements about grief.
If you agree with the statement, draw one heart next to it.
If you really, really agree with it, draw two hearts next to it.
If you do not agree, draw an X next to it.

1. It's okay to cry when you feel sad.

2. It's normal to be upset and worried when someone you love has died.

3. Everyone grieves the same way.

4. I know it's okay to tell someone that I don't feel well because I am grieving.

5. I will miss _____ for a long time.

6. I can be happy again, even though _____ had died.

7. Hiding my feelings is a good way to feel better.

8. My positive thoughts help me feel better.

9. Hurting myself or others in school or at home is a good way to express grief.

10. Taking time to breath and relax helps me when I feel upset.

Activity 27

Dear _____

_____

_____

_____

_____

_____

_____

_____

_____

Love Always,

_____

Activity 28

©2014 Kids' Grief Relief

Dear _____

_____

_____

_____

_____

_____

_____

_____

_____

_____

_____

Love Always,

_____

Activity 29

FOREVER CALENDAR

During each and every day,
We Love them.

During each and every night,
We Love them.

During each and every week,
We Love them.

During each and every month,
We Love them.

During each and every season,
We Love them.

During each and every year,
We Love them.

As the days turn into weeks, turn into months,
turn into seasons, turn into years,
We Love them;
Forever.

Activity 30

Bye Kids! I'm leaving you these powerful Heart—Words to say anytime you're feeling some grief.

Say thes words over and over until you begin to feel the POWER inside you. Then go ahead and have a great day !

The Power of my heart is strong
It gently guides me all day long.
If I feel sad throughout the day
This Love reminds me, **I'm still okay!**

Even though my life has changed
Since _____ has gone away,
There is one thing that's always there
It's Love inside my heart to share.

Activity 31A

I AM A POWERFUL KID !

www.ingramcontent.com/pod-product-compliance
Lightning Source LLC
LaVergne TN
LVHW072108070426
835509LV00002B/71